Knitted Scarves
Lace, Cables, and Textures

SHERYL THIES

Martingale®
Create with Confidence

Knitted Scarves: Lace, Cables, and Textures
© 2014 by Sheryl Thies

Martingale®
19021 120th Ave. NE, Ste. 102
Bothell, WA 98011-9511 USA
ShopMartingale.com

Printed in China

19 18 17 16 15 14   8 7 6 5 4 3 2 1

Library of Congress Cataloging-in-Publication Data is available upon request.

ISBN: 978-1-60468-503-9

Projects in this book have been published previously in *Ocean Breezes* by Sheryl Thies (Martingale, 2007).

Mission Statement
Dedicated to providing quality products and service to inspire creativity.

Contents

Fish Net

Fish Net

Fish Net can be used in so many ways. Tie on a few shells and use it as a decorative wall hanging. Tie it around your waist as a partial beach cover-up. Or simply drape it around your neck or head as a stylish scarf.

Finished Measurements
Approx 7" x 78"

Materials
1 skein of Bamboo from South West Trading
    Company (100% bamboo; 100 g; 250 yds) in color
    521 Chocolate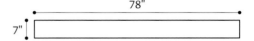
Size 8 needles or size required to obtain gauge
Size 10½ needles for bind off

Gauge
Approx 20 sts = 4" in fish net patt on size 8 needles

Fish Net Pattern
(Odd number of sts)
    Row 1: K1, *YO, sl 1, K1, pass YO and sl st tog over knit st, rep from *.
    Row 2: P1, *YO, P1, rep from *.
    Rep rows 1 and 2 for patt.

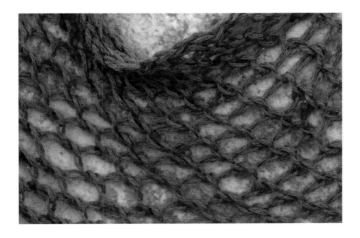

Scarf
CO 35 sts and knit 2 rows.
    Work in fish net patt until piece measures approx 78", ending with row 2.
    Knit 2 rows.
    With 10½ needles, BO all sts very loosely.

Finishing
Weave in ends. Block, using the pin-and-mist method (page 31) to smooth and even sts.

```
        |←————————— 78" —————————→|
     ┌  ┌──────────────────────────┐
  7" │  │                          │
     └  └──────────────────────────┘
```

Design Option
To make a wall hanging approximately 20" wide, purchase an additional ball of yarn and CO 100 sts; work to desired length. Tie on shells for additional embellishment.

Kelp Forest

Kelp Forest

Kelp forests provide habitats for sea creatures and even help reduce the chop from the afternoon winds that surfers complain about. The fancy rib seaweed pattern makes a nice scarf for men and women, boys and girls.

Finished Measurements
Approx 5" x 55"

Materials
3 skeins of Premiere from Classic Elite Yarns (50% pima cotton, 50% tencel; 50 g; 108 yds) in color 5297 Wood Fern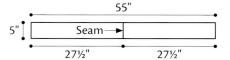
Size 6 needles or size required to obtain gauge
Stitch holder
Tapestry needle

Gauge
28 sts = 4" in seaweed st patt, slightly stretched

Seaweed Stitch Pattern
(Multiple of 6 sts)

Row 1 (WS): *P4, K2, rep from *.

Row 2 and all RS rows: Knit the knit sts and purl the purl sts as they face you.

Row 3: *P3, K3, rep from *.

Row 5: *P2, K4, rep from *.

Row 7: P1, *K4, P2, rep from * to last 5 sts, K4, P1.

Row 9: P1, *K3, P3, rep from * to last 5 sts, K3, P2.

Row 11: P1, *K2, P4, rep from * to last 5 sts, K2, P3.

Row 12: Knit the knit sts and purl the purl sts as they face you.

Rep rows 1–12 for patt.

Scarf
Make 2 pieces.

CO 36 sts. Work in seaweed st patt until piece measures approx 27½", ending with row 12.

Purl 1 row. Place all sts on st holder.

Make second piece and leave sts on needles.

Finishing
Place sts from holder onto knitting needle. Graft 2 pieces tog, using Kitchener st (page 29). Weave in ends. Block using the mist method (page 31) to smooth and even sts.

Design Option
For an 8"-wide scarf, CO 48 sts and work as directed to desired length. You'll need 2 additional skeins of yarn.

Mermaid Mesh

Mermaid Mesh

Tales of mermaids are universal and have enticed the human race for centuries. Delight your little mermaid with a scarf stitched in this magical mesh lace pattern.

Finished Measurements

Approx 5" x 55"

Materials

2 skeins of String of Pearls from Muench (70% cotton, 20% rayon, 10% polyester; 50 g; 99 yds) in color 4004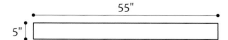

Size 10½ needles or size required to obtain gauge

Gauge

17 sts = 4" in mermaid mesh patt, slightly stretched

Mermaid Mesh Pattern

(Multiple of 9 + 4 sts)

Row 1: Purl.

Row 2 (RS): K1, YO, *(ssk, YO) 3 times, K3tog, YO twice, rep from * to last 3 sts, ssk, K1.

Row 3 and all WS rows: Purl, working "YO twice" as K1, P1.

Row 4: *K2tog, YO twice, (ssk, YO) twice, K3tog, YO, rep from * to last 4 sts, K2tog, YO, K2.

Row 6: K1, *K2tog, YO twice, ssk, YO, K3tog, YO, K2tog, YO, rep from * to last 3 sts, K2tog, YO, K1.

Row 8: K2tog, YO, *K2tog, YO twice, sl 1, K2tog, psso, (YO, K2tog) twice, YO, rep from * to last 2 sts, K2.

Row 10: K1, K2tog, YO, *K2tog, YO twice, sl 1, K2tog, psso, (YO, K2tog) twice, YO, rep from * to last st, K1.

Row 12: K2tog, YO, *K2tog, YO twice, ssk, YO, sl 1, K2tog, psso, YO, K2tog, YO, rep from * to last 2 sts, K2.

Row 14: K1, K2tog, *YO twice, (ssk, YO) twice, sl 1, K2tog, psso, YO, K2tog, rep from * to last st, YO, K1.

Row 16: K2tog, *YO twice, (ssk, YO) 3 times, K3tog, rep from * to last 2 sts, YO twice, ssk.

Rep rows 1–16 for patt.

Scarf

CO 22 sts and work in mermaid mesh patt until piece measures approx 55", ending with row 1.

Loosely BO all sts purlwise.

Finishing

Weave in ends. Block using the damp-towel method (page 31) to smooth and even sts.

55"

5"

Design Options

Wear this garment as a sash wrapped around your waist. Or, for a 15"-wide scarf, CO 66 sts and work as directed. You'll need 6 skeins of yarn for this wider version.

Ocean Currents

Ocean Currents

Complex ocean currents are created by the constant movement of the water. This attractive stitch pattern conveys the graceful motion of water, while the soft shimmer of the silk yarn calls to mind the glistening surface of the ocean.

Finished Measurements
Approx 6" x 50"

Materials
2 skeins of Regal Silk from Art Yarns (100% silk; 50 g; 163 yds) in color 115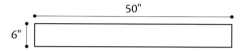

Size 6 needles or size required to obtain gauge

Gauge
30 sts = 4" in ocean current patt

Ocean Current Pattern
(Patt worked over 37 sts plus 8 edge sts)

Row 1 (RS): K4, YO, K10, K2tog tbl, K9, K2tog, K9, YO, K5, K4.

Row 2: K4, P6, YO, P9, P2tog, P7, P2tog tbl, P10, YO, P1, K4.

Row 3: K4, K2, YO, K10, K2tog tbl, K5, K2tog, K9, YO, K7, K4.

Row 4: K4, P8, YO, P9, P2tog, P3, P2tog tbl, P10, YO, P3, K4.

Row 5: K4, K4, YO, K10, K2tog tbl, K1, K2tog, K9, YO, K9, K4.

Row 6: K4, YO, P9, P2tog, P9, P2tog tbl, P10, YO, P5, K4.

Row 7: K4, K6, YO, K10, K2tog tbl, K7, K2tog, K9, YO, K1, K4.

Row 8: K4, P2, YO, P9, P2tog, P5, P2tog tbl, P10, YO, P7, K4.

Row 9: K4, K8, YO, K10, K2tog tbl, K3, K2tog, K9, YO, K3, K4.

Row 10: K4, P4, YO, P9, P2tog, P1, P2tog tbl, P10, YO, P9, K4.

Rep rows 1–10 for patt.

Scarf
CO 45 sts and knit 6 rows.

Work in ocean current patt until piece measures approx 49", ending with row 10.

Knit 6 rows.

BO all sts loosely.

Finishing
Weave in ends. Block using the pin-and-mist method (page 31) to smooth and even sts.

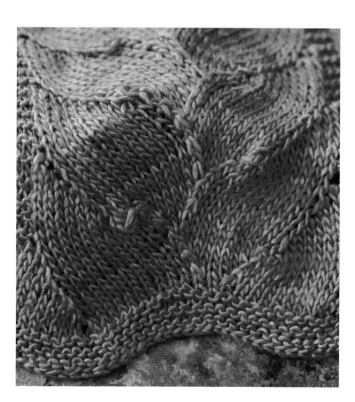

Scallop Shells

Scallop Shells

The scallop is probably best known for its beautiful and distinctive shell with radiating ribs, which has inspired artists for centuries. Let the shell inspire you to work this lace-and-wrap-stitch scarf.

Finished Measurements
Approx 7" x 64"

Materials
3 skeins of Svale from Dale of Norway (50% cotton, 40% viscose, 10% silk; 50 g; 114 yds) in color 5403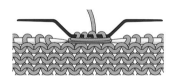
Size 4 needles or size required to obtain gauge
Cable needle
Stitch holder

Gauge
29 sts = 4" in scallop shell patt

Scallop Shell Pattern
(Multiple of 21 + 9 sts)

P4wrap: P4 and sl those sts to cn, wrap yarn counterclockwise around 4 slipped sts 3 times, sl 4 sts back to right-hand needle.

Row 1 (WS): Knit.
Row 2 (RS): K3, purl to last 3 sts, K3.
Row 3: Knit.
Row 4: K4, *YO, K21, rep from * to last 5 sts, K5—53 sts.
Row 5: K3, P3, *(K3, P1) 5 times, P2, rep from * to last 3 sts, K3.
Row 6: K5, *YO, K1, (P3, K1) 5 times, YO, K1, rep from * to last 4 sts, K4—57 sts.
Row 7: K3, *P4, (K3, P1) 5 times, rep from * to last 6 sts, P3, K3.

Row 8: K5, *YO, K1, YO, (ssk, P2) 5 times, (K1, YO) twice, K1, rep from * to last 4 sts, K4—55 sts.
Row 9: K3, *P6, (K2, P1) 5 times, P2, rep from * to last 6 sts, P3, K3.
Row 10: K5, *(YO, K1) 3 times, YO, (ssk, P1) 5 times, (K1, YO) 4 times, K1, rep from * to last 4 sts, K4—61 sts.
Row 11: K3, *P10, (K1, P1) 5 times, P6, rep from * to last 6 sts, P3, K3.
Row 12: K4, *K8, ssk 5 times, K8, rep from * to last 5 sts, K5—51 sts.
Row 13: K3, *P10, P4wrap, P7, rep from * to last 6 sts, P3, K3.
Row 14: Knit.
Rep rows 1–14 for patt.

Scarf
Make 2 pieces.

CO 51 sts and work in scallop shell patt until piece measures approx 32", ending with row 14.
Sl all sts to st holder.
Make second piece and leave on needle.

Finishing
Place sts from holder onto knitting needle. Graft the 2 pieces tog using Kitchener st (page 29). Weave in ends. Block using the mist method (page 31) to smooth and even sts.

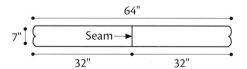

Sea Cucumbers

Sea Cucumbers

All deep sea divers know that sea cucumbers are not really vegetables and not really a delicacy, but this scarf is pure indulgence. The pattern stitch is an uncomplicated rhythmic pattern of knits and purls that is quickly memorized.

Finished Measurements
Approx 6" x 98"

Materials
4 skeins of Inca Alpaca from Classic Elite (100% alpaca; 50 g; 100 m/109 yds) in color 1109 **4**
Size 7 needles or size required to obtain gauge

Gauge
20 sts = 4" in sea cucumber patt

Sea Cucumber Pattern
(Multiple of 8 + 6 sts, + 8 edge sts)
Row 1 (RS): K4, K4, P2, *K6, P2, rep from * to last 4 sts, K4.
Row 2: K4, P1, K2, *P6, K2, rep from * to last 7 sts, P3, K4.
Row 3: *K6, P2, rep from * to last 6 sts, K6.
Row 4: K4, P3, K2, *P6, K2, rep from * to last 5 sts, P1, K4.
Row 5: K4, P2, *K6, P2, rep from * to last 8 sts, K8.
Row 6: K4, purl to last 4 sts, K4.
Row 7: Knit.
Row 8: K4, purl to last 4 sts, K4.
Rep rows 1–8 for patt.

Scarf
CO 30 sts and knit 7 rows.
Next row: K4, purl to last 4 sts, K4.
Work in sea cucumber patt until piece measures approx 96", ending with row 8.
Knit 7 rows.
BO all sts loosely purlwise.

Finishing
Weave in ends. Block using the mist method (page 31) to smooth and even sts.

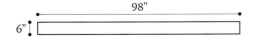

Design Option
You will have enough yarn for a wider but shorter scarf. CO 46 sts for a finished piece that is 9¼" x 60".

Sea Foam

Sea Foam

It's hard to believe this delicate and lacy fabric is made by just knitting. The yarn overs create elongated stitches that add the openwork. This is an easy pattern, even if you've never worked lace before.

Finished Measurements
Approx 14" x 78"

Materials
2 skeins of Gossamer from Karabella Yarns (52% nylon, 30% kid mohair, 18% polyester; 50 g/1.78 oz; 200 m/222 yds) in color 6105 Ice Blue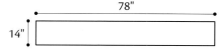
Size 9 needles or size required to obtain gauge

Gauge
13 sts = 4" in sea foam patt

Sea Foam Pattern
(Multiple of 10 + 4 sts)
Row 1 (RS): Knit.
Row 2: Knit.
Row 3: K10, *YO twice, K1, YO 3 times, K1, YO 4 times, K1, YO 3 times, K1, YO twice, K6, rep from * to last 4 sts, K4.
Row 4: Knit across, dropping all YOs off needle.
Rows 5 and 6: Knit.

Row 7: K5, *YO twice, K1, YO 3 times, K1, YO 4 times, K1, YO 3 times, K1, YO twice, K6, rep from *, end last repeat with K5 instead of K6.
Row 8: Knit across, dropping all YOs off needle.
Rep rows 1–8 for patt.

Scarf
CO 44 sts and knit 2 rows.
Work in sea foam patt until piece measures approx 77½", ending with row 8.
Knit 4 rows.
BO all sts loosely.

Finishing
Weave in all ends. Block using the wet-blocking method (page 31) to smooth and even sts. You may have to use your hands to extend elongated sts as you pin in place.

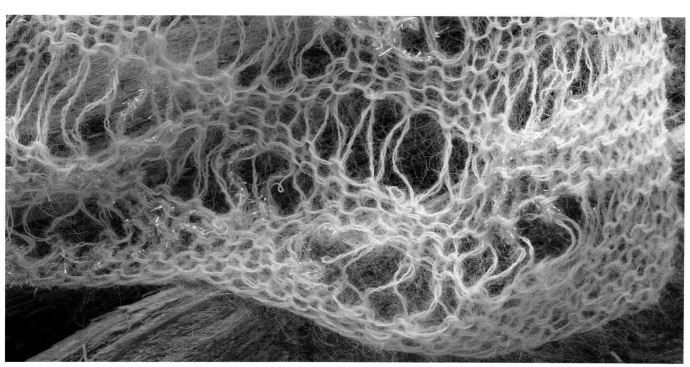

Sea Horses

Sea Horses

The sea horse is actually a fish with a horse-shaped head. Its colors are variable but this scarf portrays red sea horses, made with a cable stitch, hiding in coral lace. The entire piece is edged in a picot crochet stitch that is easy to work.

Finished Measurements
Approx 14" x 64" (including crochet edge)

Materials
8 skeins of Cotton Twist from Berroco (70% cotton, 30% rayon; 50 g/1.75 oz; 78 m/85 yds) in color 8311

Size 9 circular (36") needle or size required to obtain gauge
Size 10½ needles for bind off
Cable needle
Size I-9 (5.5 mm) crochet hook

Gauge
13 sts = 4" in sea horse patt on size 9 needle after blocking

Sea Horse Pattern
(Patt multiple of 8 plus 4 edge sts)
    Row 1 (RS): K2, *K4, YO, K2tog, YO, K2tog, * rep from * to last 2 sts, K2.
    Row 2 and all WS rows: K2, purl to last 2 sts, K2.
    Row 3: K2, *K4, YO, K2tog, YO, K2tog, rep from * to last 2 sts, K2.

Row 5: K2, *sl 2 to cn and hold at front, K2, K2 from cn, YO, K2tog, YO, K2tog, rep from * to last 2 sts, K2.

Row 7: K2, *K4, YO, K2tog, YO, K2tog, rep from * to last 2 sts, K2.

Row 9: K2, *YO, K2tog, YO, K2tog, K4, rep from * to last 2 sts, K2.

Row 11: K2, *YO, K2tog, YO, K2tog, K4, rep from * to last 2 sts, K2.

Row 13: K2, *YO, K2tog, YO, K2tog, sl 2 to cn and hold at back, K2, K2 from cn, rep from * to last 2 sts, K2.

Row 15: K2, *YO, K2tog, YO, K2tog, K4, rep from * to last 2 sts, K2.

Row 16: K2, purl to last 2 sts, K2.
Rep rows 1–16 for patt.

Scarf

Using cable cast on (see box, below), loosely CO 204 sts. Knit 1 row.

Work a total of 6 sea horse patt reps.
Knit 1 row.
With size 10½ needles, loosely BO all sts purlwise.

Picot Crochet Edge

Row 1: Sc around all edges, working 3 sc in corner sts.

Row 2: Ch 1, work 2 sc in each of next 2 sc, *ch 4, sl st in first ch of ch 4 (picot made), sc in each of next 3 sc, rep from * to last st, work 2 sc in last st, join with sl st. Fasten off.

Finishing

Weave in ends. Block using the pin-and-mist method (page 31) to smooth and even sts.

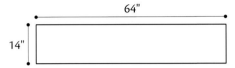

Measurements include crochet edge.

Cable cast on: Make a slipknot and place on needle. Knit into stitch and place resulting stitch on left needle by inserting left needle into stitch from right side of loop. *Insert right needle between two stitches, wrap yarn around needle, pull new loop through to front, and place on left needle. Repeat from * for specified number of stitches.

Insert needle between two stitches. Knit a stitch.

Place new stitch on left needle.

Turtle Tracks

Travel on shore is awkward for turtles, and they leave a very distinctive track in the sand. This turtle-track pattern is edged with vertical garter-stitch scallops and delicately knotted fringe.

Finished Measurements
Approx 13" to 15" x 66" (without fringe)

Materials
6 skeins of Dune from Trendsetter Yarns (36% mohair, 35% cotton, 15% nylon, 12% acrylic, 2% metal; 50 g; 82 yds) in color 115
Size 10½ needles or size required to obtain gauge
Size I-9 (5.5 mm) crochet hook

Gauge
12 sts = 4" in turtle tracks patt

Turtle Tracks Pattern with Scalloped Edge
(Worked over 41 sts)
    Row 1 (WS): K1, K1f&b, K5, P6, K3, P9, K3, P6, K5, K1f&b, K1—43 sts.
    Row 2 (RS): K1, K1f&b, K12, P3, YO, K4, ssk, K3, P3, K12, K1f&b, K1—45 sts.

Turtle Tracks

Row 3: K1, K1f&b, K7, P6, K3, P9, K3, P6, K7, K1f&b, K1—47 sts.

Row 4: K1, K1f&b, K14, P3, K1, YO, K4, ssk, K2, P3, K14, K1f&b, K1—49 sts.

Row 5: K1, K1f&b, K9, P6, K3, P9, K3, P6, K9, K1f&b, K1—51 sts.

Row 6: K1, K1f&b, K16, P3, K2, YO, K4, ssk, K1, P3, K16, K1f&b, K1—53 sts.

Row 7: K1, K1f&b, K11, P6, K3, P9, K3, P6, K11, K1f&b, K1—55 sts.

Row 8: K1, K1f&b, K18, P3, K3, YO, K4, ssk, P3, K18, K1f&b, K1—57 sts.

Row 9: K1, ssk, K12, P6, K3, P9, K3, P6, K12, K2tog, K1—55 sts.

Row 10: K1, ssk, K17, P3, K3, K2tog, K4, YO, P3, K17, K2tog, K1—53 sts.

Row 11: K1, ssk, K10, P6, K3, P9, K3, P6, K10, K2tog, K1—51 sts.

Row 12: K1, ssk, K15, P3, K2, K2tog, K4, YO, K1, P3, K15, K2tog, K1—49 sts.

Row 13: K1, ssk, K8, P6, K3, P9, K3, P6, K8, K2tog, K1—47 sts.

Row 14: K1, ssk, K13, P3, K1, K2tog, K4, YO, K2, P3, K13, K2tog, K1—45 sts.

Row 15: K1, ssk, K6, P6, K3, P9, K3, P6, K6, K2tog, K1—43 sts.

Row 16: K1, ssk, K11, P3, K2tog, K4, YO, K3, P3, K11, K2tog, K1—41 sts.

Rep rows 1–16 for patt.

Scarf

CO 41 sts and knit 1 row.

Work in turtle tracks patt until piece measures approx 66", ending with row 1.

Knit 1 row.

BO all sts loosely.

Finishing

Weave in ends. Block using the mist method (page 31) to smooth and even sts.

Fringe: Cut 16 strands of yarn, each 24" long. Using crochet hook, attach 8 single strands of fringe (page 29) along each bottom edge as shown below. Using overhand knot, make 2 rows of knots as shown below.

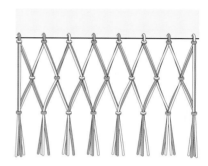

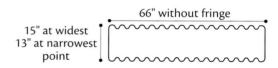

15" at widest
13" at narrowest point

66" without fringe

Nautical Twisted Rope

Nautical Twisted Rope

Walk along the docks and you'll see coils of bulky weathered rope. This scarf conveys the old sea touch that any sailor will admire. The bold cable pattern appears complex but works up quickly.

Finished Measurements

Approx 8" x 56"

Materials

2 skeins of Cascade 220 from Cascade Yarns (100% Peruvian Highland wool; 100 g/3.5 oz; 220 yds) in color 8013

Size 8 needles or size required to obtain gauge

Cable needle

Gauge

24 sts = 4" in nautical cable patt, slightly stretched

Nautical Cable Pattern

(Worked over 49 sts)

Front cross (FC): Sl 2 sts to cn and hold at front, K2, K2 from cn.

Back cross (BC): Sl 2 sts to cn and hold at back, K2, K2 from cn.

Row 1 (RS): (P2, K4) 4 times, P1, (K4, P2) 4 times.

Rows 2, 4, 6, and 8: (K2, P4) 4 times, K1, (P4, K2) 4 times.

Row 3: (P2, FC, P2, K4) twice, P1, (K4, P2, BC, P2) twice.

Row 5: (P2, K4) 4 times, P1, (K4, P2) 4 times.

Row 7: P2, FC, P2, K4, P2, FC, P2, sl 5 sts to cn and hold at front, K4, sl purl st from cn to left needle and purl it, K4 from cn, P2, BC, P2, K4, P2, BC, P2.

Row 9: P2, K4, P2, M1, (K4, P2) twice, K4, M1, P1, M1, (K4, P2) twice, K4, M1, P2, K4, P2—53 sts.

Row 10: K2, P4, *K3, P4, (K2, P4) twice, rep from * once, K3, P4, K2.

Row 11: P2, FC, P3, M1, K4, P2tog, FC, P2tog, K4, M1, P3, M1, K4, P2tog, BC, P2tog, K4, M1, P3, BC, P2.

Row 12: K2, P4, K4, (P4, K1) twice, P4, K5, (P4, K1) twice, P4, K4, P4, K2.

Row 13: P2, K4, P4, M1, K3, ssk, K4, K2tog, K3, M1, P5, M1, K3, ssk, K4, K2tog, K3, M1, P4, K4, P2.

Row 14: K2, P4, K5, P12, K7, P12, K5, P4, K2.

Row 15: P2, FC, P5, M1, K4, FC, K4, M1, P7, M1, K4, BC, K4, M1, P5, BC, P2—57 sts.

Row 16: K2, P4, K6, P12, K9, P12, K6, P4, K2.

Row 17: P2, K4, P6, sl 8 sts to cn and hold at back, K4, sl second 4 sts from cn to left needle and knit them, K4 from cn, P9, sl 8 sts to cn and hold at front, K4, sl second 4 sts from cn to left needle and knit them, K4 from cn, P6, K4, P2.

Row 18: K2, P4, K6, P12, K9, P12, K6, P4, K2.

Row 19: P2, FC, P4, P2tog, K4, FC, K4, P2tog, P5, P2tog, K4, BC, K4, P2tog, P4, BC, P2—53 sts.

Row 20: K2, P4, K5, P12, K7, P12, K5, P4, K2.

Row 21: P2, K4, P3, *P2tog, (K4, M1) twice, K4, P2tog, P3, rep from * once, K4, P2.

Row 22: K2, P4, K4, (P4, K1) twice, P4, K5, (P4, K1) twice, P4, K4, P4, K2.

Row 23: P2, FC, P2, P2tog, K4, M1, P1, FC, P1, M1, K4, P2tog, P1, P2tog, K4, M1, P1, BC, P1, M1, K4, P2tog, P2, BC, P2.

Row 24: K2, P4, *K3, P4, (K2, P4) twice, rep from * once, K3, P4, K2.

Row 25: P2, K4, P1, P2tog, (K4, P2) twice, K4, P3tog, (K4, P2) twice, K4, P2tog, P1, K4, P2—49 sts.

Row 26: (K2, P4) 4 times, K1, (P4, K2) 4 times.

Row 27: P2, FC, P2, K4, P2, FC, P2, sl 5 sts to cn and hold at front, K4, sl purl st from cn to left needle and purl it, K4 from cn, P2, BC, P2, K4, P2, BC, P2.

Row 28: (K2, P4) 4 times, K1, (P4, K2) 4 times.

Rep rows 1–28 for patt.

Scarf

CO 49 sts and work in nautical cable patt until piece measures approx 56", ending with row 2.

BO all sts in patt loosely.

Finishing

Weave in ends. Block using the mist method (page 31) to smooth and even sts.

56"

8"

Goldfish Tails

Goldfish Tails

The fishtail lace pattern is as mesmerizing as watching goldfish in an aquarium. The bobble trim accentuates and outlines the fishtails, and the L shape means this scarf will stay on.

Finished Measurements
Approx 39" x 39" (along outside edges of L shape)

Materials
Approx 800 yds of hand-dyed 100% merino sock
   yarn
Size 10 needles or size required to obtain gauge
Tapestry needle

Gauge
17 sts = 4" in fish-tail lace patt

Bottom Bobble Edge
(Multiple of 6 + 5 sts)

   MB (make bobble): (K1f&b twice, K1) in same st, turn, K5, turn, P5, turn, K5, turn; sl 2nd, 3rd, 4th, and 5th st over first st, K1.

   Row 1 (WS): Knit.

   Row 2 (RS): K2, *MB, K5, rep from * to last 3 sts, MB, K2.

   Row 3: Knit.

Fishtail Lace Pattern with Bobble-Edge Sides

(Multiple of 8 + 1 sts, + 10 sts for bobble-edge sides)

Row 1 (RS): K6, *YO, K2, sl 1, K2tog, psso, K2, YO, K1, rep from * to last 5 sts, K5.

Row 2 and all WS rows: K5, purl to last 5 sts, K5.

Row 3: K2, MB, K4, *YO, K1, sl 1, K2tog, psso, K1, YO, K3, rep from * to last 12 sts, YO, K1, sl 1, K2tog, psso, K1, YO, K4, MB, K2.

Row 5: K8, *YO, sl 1, K2tog, psso, YO, K5, rep from * to last 11 sts, YO, sl 1, K2tog, psso, YO, K8.

Row 6: K5, purl to last 5 sts, K5.

Rep rows 1–6 for patt.

If using hand-dyed yarn, work from 2 balls of yarn at the same time to achieve an even color effect. Work 2 rows from 1 ball, then 2 rows from second ball. Do not cut yarn; instead, carry yarn up side of work.

Piece A

CO 65 sts and work rows 1–3 of bottom bobble edge, inc 2 sts evenly across last row—67 sts.

Work in fishtail lace patt until piece measures approx 39", slightly stretched, ending with row 6.

Knit 1 row and dec 2 sts evenly across row—65 sts.

Work rows 1–3 of bottom bobble edge. BO all sts loosely.

Piece B

Work as for piece A until piece measures approx 24", slightly stretched, ending with row 6.

Knit 2 rows.

BO all sts loosely.

Finishing

With RS facing you, sew BO edge of B to side edge of A as shown below. Weave in all ends. Block using the pin-and-mist method (page 31) to smooth and even sts.

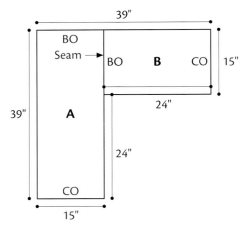

Design Option

For a more subdued look, you can eliminate the bobbles along the side edges of the fishtail lace pattern by working a knit stitch in place of make bobble.

Techniques

Following are a few of the techniques used in this book.

Fringe: Cut fringe to the specified length. Fold fringe in half. Insert crochet hook from front to back of work. Catch the folded fringe and pull through the knitted piece, creating a loop. Draw fringe ends through the loop and pull to tighten. Trim as necessary to even lengths.

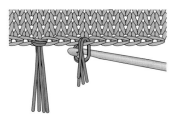

Joining a new ball of yarn: Whenever possible, attach a new ball of yarn at the beginning of the row. Tie the new strand onto the old tail with a single knot. Slide the new knot up the old tail to the needle and begin knitting with the new yarn. Weave in the tails when you finish the project.

Kitchener stitch: Place the stitches to be grafted onto two needles and fasten off the working yarn. Thread a tapestry needle with a length of yarn approximately three times the width of the seam. Hold the two knitting needles together in the left hand with the points facing to the right and the wrong sides of the knitting facing together. Hold the threaded tapestry needle in the right hand.

1. Go through the first stitch on the front needle as if to purl and leave it on the needle. Go through the first stitch on the back needle as if to knit and leave it on the needle.

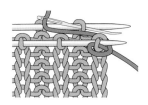

2. Go through the first stitch on the front needle as if to knit and slip it off the needle. Go through the second stitch on the front needle as if to purl and leave it on the needle.
3. Go through the first stitch on the back needle as if to purl and slip it off the needle. Go through the second stitch on the back needle as if to knit and leave it on the needle.

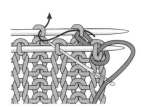

Here's a shortcut to help you remember what to do:

Front needle: Knit off, purl on.
Back needle: Purl off, knit on.

Repeat steps 2 and 3 until all stitches are joined, adjusting tension to match the tension of the knitted work.

Yarn over (YO): If the last stitch worked is a knit stitch, bring the yarn between the two needles to the front. Take the yarn over the right-hand needle to the back: one yarn over made. If the last stitch worked is a purl stitch, the yarn is already in the front. Take the yarn over the right-hand needle to the back: one yarn over made. After the yarn over, if the next stitch to be worked is a knit stitch, the yarn is already in position to work. If the next stitch to be worked is a purl st, bring the yarn between the needles to the front. For multiple yarn overs, repeat for the desired number of yarn overs.

Knit in row below: Knit into the center of the stitch below the next stitch on the left needle and drop the stitch above off the left needle.

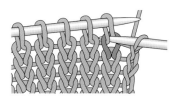

Crochet

Chain (ch): Wrap yarn around hook and pull through loop on hook.

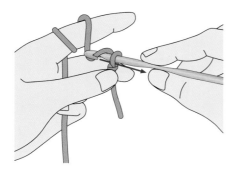

Crab stitch (or reverse single crochet): Work a row of single crochet along edge with right side facing you. At the end of the row, *do not turn work.* Work a row of crab stitch from left to right. Insert hook into first stitch to the right, yarn over hook, and pull through both loops on hook. Repeat around; join and fasten off.

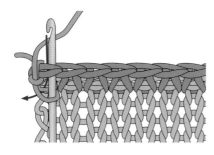

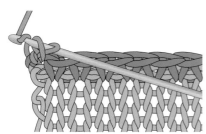

Double crochet (dc): Working from right to left with right side facing you, yarn over hook, insert hook into next stitch, yarn over hook, and pull loop to front (three loops on hook). Yarn over hook and pull through first two loops on hook (two loops remain on hook). Yarn over hook and pull through remaining two loops (one loop remains on hook).

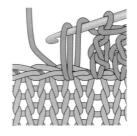

Yarn over hook, insert hook into stitch, yarn over hook, pull through to front.

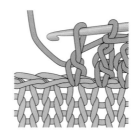

Yarn over hook, pull through two loops on hook.

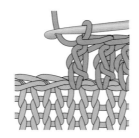

Yarn over hook, pull through remaining two loops on hook.

Single crochet (sc): Working from right to left with right side facing you, insert the hook into next stitch, yarn over hook, pull loop to front, yarn over hook, and pull loop through both loops on hook. Space stitches so the edge lies flat.

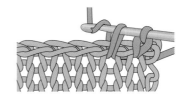

Insert hook into stitch, yarn over hook, pull loop through to front, yarn over hook.

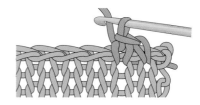

Pull loop through both loops on hook.

The formula for spacing stitches on a vertical edge is to work into each knot at the edge. For a horizontal row, the formula is every one and one-half stitches. However, even using the formulas as a guide, it may be necessary to skip or add stitches to keep the edge flat.

When working a crochet edge on a knitted piece, always begin by working a row of single crochet to stabilize the edges. To work additional rows of single crochet, insert the hook under both loops of the stitch below, and then work one single crochet into each stitch in the previous row.

Slip stitch (sl st): Working from right to left with right side facing you, insert hook into next stitch, yarn over hook, pull loop through stitch, and in one continuous motion, draw it through the loop on the hook.

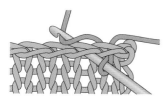

Insert hook into stitch, yarn over hook.

Pull loop of yarn through stitch and loop on hook.

Blocking

First choose a flat waterproof surface to spread out the piece to be blocked. You can purchase blocking boards for this purpose. The top on an ironing board works well for smaller pieces, or the floor covered with a towel also works. Regardless of the method used for blocking, the piece should remain in place until dry.

Damp-towel method: Lay the knitted piece on the surface, shaping to specified dimensions. Dampen a towel, large enough to cover the knitted piece; running a saturated towel through the spin cycle of the washing machine works well. Place the damp towel over the knitted piece for 1 to 2 hours. Remove the towel, but leave the piece to dry completely before moving it.

Mist method: Lay the knitted piece on the surface, shaping to specified dimensions. Fill a clean spray bottle with water and mist the piece lightly with water. Allow to dry completely before moving it.

Pin-and-mist method: Lay the knitted piece on the surface and pin to specified measurements. Fill a clean spray bottle with water and mist the piece heavily with water. Allow to dry completely before removing pins.

Wet-blocking method: Dip knitted piece in cool water. Gently squeeze out the water. Do not wring or twist the piece. Roll the piece in an absorbent bath towel to blot out the excess water. Spread the piece on the surface and pin to specified dimensions. Allow to dry completely before removing pins.

Standard Yarn-Weight System

Yarn-Weight Symbol and Category Name	1 Super Fine	2 Fine	3 Light	4 Medium	5 Bulky	6 Super Bulky
Types of Yarn in Category	Sock, Fingering, Baby	Sport, Baby	DK, Light Worsted	Worsted, Afghan, Aran	Chunky, Craft, Rug	Bulky, Roving
Knit Gauge* Range in Stockinette Stitch to 4"	27 to 32 sts	23 to 26 sts	21 to 24 sts	16 to 20 sts	12 to 15 sts	6 to 11 sts
Recommended Needle in US Size Range	1 to 3	3 to 5	5 to 7	7 to 9	9 to 11	11 and larger
Recommended Needle in Metric Size Range	2.25 to 3.25 mm	3.25 to 3.75 mm	3.75 to 4.5 mm	4.5 to 5.5 mm	5.5 to 8 mm	8 mm and larger

*These are guidelines only. The above reflect the most commonly used gauges and hook sizes for specific yarn categories.

Abbreviations and Glossary

approx	approximately
beg	begin(ning)
BO	bind off
ch	chain
cn	cable needle
CO	cast on
cont	continue
dc	double crochet
dec	decrease
g	grams
inc	increase
K1f&b	knit into front and back of same stitch—1 stitch increased
K	knit
K2tog	knit 2 sts together—1 stitch decreased
K3tog	knit 3 stitches together—2 stitches decreased
M1	make 1 stitch: Insert the left needle from front to back under strand between last stitch worked and next stitch on left needle. Knit this lifted strand through the back loop—1 stitch increased.
m	meter
oz	ounces
P	purl
P2tog	purl 2 stitches together—1 stitch decreased
P3tog	purl 3 stitches together—2 stitches decreased
patt	pattern
pm	place marker

psso	pass slipped stitch over
p2sso	pass 2 slipped stitches over
PU	pick up and knit
rem	remain(s)(ing)
rep(s)	repeat(s)
RS	right side
sc	single crochet
sk	skip
sl	slip
sl st	slip stitch: slip 1 stitch purlwise with yarn in back unless otherwise instructed
sl 1, K2tog, psso	slip 1 stitch as if to knit, knit 2 stitches together, pass slipped stitch over—2 stitches decreased
sl 2, K1, p2sso	slip 2 stitches together as if to knit, knit 1 stitch, pass 2 slipped stitches over—2 stitches decreased
ssk	slip, slip, knit: Slip 2 stitches separately as if to knit. Insert left needle into these 2 stitches from left to right and knit them together through the back loops—1 stitch decreased.
st(s)	stitch(es)
tbl	through back loop
tog	together
WS	wrong side
wyib	with yarn in back
wyif	with yarn in front
yds	yards
YO	yarn over